OPENING

D0933821

WITHDRAWN

George Washington Carver

Innovator in Agriculture

Lisa Halvorsen

BLACKBIRCH®
PRESS

THOMSON
GALE

San Diego • Detroit • New York • San Francisco • Cleveland
New Haven, Conn. • Waterville, Maine • London • Munich

LIBRARY OF CONGRESS CATALOGING-IN-PUBLICATION DATA

Halvorsen, Lisa.
 George Washington Carver / by Lisa Halvorsen.
  p. cm. — (Giants of science series)
Summary: Discusses the birth, education, opportunities, agricultural career, innovations, promotions, and legacy of George Washington Carver.
Includes bibliographical references (p. 63).
 ISBN 1-56711-657-4 (hardback : alk. paper)
 1. Carver, George Washington, 1864?-1943—Juvenile literature. 2. African American agriculturists—Biography—Juvenile literature. 3. Agriculturists—United States—Biography—Juvenile literature. [1. Carver, George Washington, 1864?-1943. 2. Agriculturists. 3. African Americans—Biography.] I. Title. II. Giants of science.
 S417.C3 H26 2003
 630'.92—dc21
2002005375

Printed in China
10 9 8 7 6 5 4 3 2 1

CONTENTS

Introduction: A Persuasive Speaker

No one paid any attention to the elderly African American in the rumpled suit who waited patiently in the back of the crowded hall. All attention was focused on the heated debate over whether or not to raise tariffs on many agricultural and industrial goods imported from foreign countries. The outcome would have a significant impact on the American economy, especially on farmers.

The members of the U.S. House of Representatives' Ways and Means Committee had already heard from several speakers. By four o'clock in the afternoon, they were tired and ready to go home. There was one more name on the docket, though—a George Washington Carver from Alabama.

The slender, slightly stooped man, who lugged two heavy wooden display cases, made his way to the front of the room. Joseph Fordney, the committee chairman, informed him that he had only ten minutes to speak. Some of the committee members began to snicker at the sight of this unlikely speaker. Carver pretended not to hear them. They laughed again when he started to speak, in a voice that had been made high-pitched by the whooping cough he had as a child. Again, he ignored them.

"Mr. Chairman, I have been asked by the United Peanut Growers' Association to tell you something about the possibility of the peanut and its possible extension," he began, as he removed samples from his case and set them on the table in front of him. "I come from Tuskegee, Alabama. I am engaged in agricultural research work, and I have given some attention to the peanut, but not as much as I expect to give."

With that, Carver launched into his testimony on the many uses of peanuts, a major economic crop in the rural South. He showed the congressmen product after product made from peanuts: candy, breakfast foods, milk, instant coffee, cooking oil, livestock feed, ink, face cream, and adhesives. He even had a use for the papery peanut skins, which, he explained, could be made into 30 different colored dyes.

When his ten minutes were up, he paused. The room remained quiet. His audience was so captivated by what he had told them that they insisted that he continue. He spoke for almost two hours and demonstrated more than 160 different products made from peanuts.

Opposite: *George Washington Carver in New York City, 1939.*

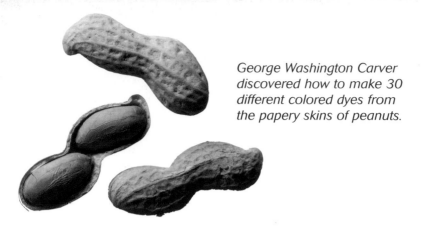

The Peanut Scientist

Although Carver spoke only about peanuts and the need for a tariff to protect this American-grown crop from foreign competition, his testimony helped lead to the passage of the Fordney-McCumber Tariff Act in 1922. This law placed a high tax on many imported agricultural and industrial commodities, including peanuts.

The law was a major victory for the United States peanut industry, and it brought fame to Carver. News of his influential presentation made headlines across the country. Suddenly, everyone wanted to hear the "peanut scientist" from Alabama speak.

This national acknowledgment of his pioneering research in chemurgy, the industrial use of agricultural products, was a turning point in Carver's life. He cared little about the personal recognition, but he was pleased by all the attention given to the scientific discoveries he had made at Tuskegee Normal and Industrial Institute for Negroes in rural Tuskegee, Alabama. It had been a long journey from his humble beginnings as a slave in Missouri.

Born a Slave

George Washington Carver was born to a slave named Mary on a farm near Diamond Grove, in southwest Missouri. Because birth records were seldom kept for slaves, his actual date of birth is not known. He was believed to have been born near the end of the Civil War, most likely in 1864. He had two sisters, both of whom died in infancy, and an older brother, Jim.

Opposite: *Carver was a pioneer in the field of using agricultural products for industrial use.*

Moses and Susan Carver, a German couple, purchased Mary in 1855 when she was only 13 years old. They paid $700 for her, although the Carvers were abolitionists and spoke out against slavery. They had no children of their own to help around the farm. They found it difficult to hire workers because land was plentiful and most able-bodied men and women, either white or freed slaves, had their own parcel of land to farm. Faced with no other choice, the Carvers decided to buy a slave.

Mary was expected to do housework, but she was treated more like a daughter than a slave. Susan was proud that Mary was a quick learner who could spin and weave faster than she herself could.

George's father was a slave on a nearby plantation. Moses tried to buy him many times, but the owner always refused because he was a hard worker who was too valuable to sell. George never knew his father—he was killed in a logging accident shortly after George was born.

A Boy for a Horse

One evening, when George was about six months old, slave raiders rode onto the Carver farm and captured him and his mother. Moses had just enough time to hide Jim behind a pile of wood. The raiders wanted to steal slaves so that they could sell them in slave markets in Arkansas, Texas, and other Southern states.

A few days after Mary and George were kidnapped, the Carvers asked a neighbor, John Bentley, to try to find them. Bentley was a former Union army scout and a good tracker. Moses offered to give Bentley one of his best horses and 40 acres of prime timberland if he could bring back the missing slaves. The horse and land together were worth almost $1,100—a large sum of money for that time.

Bentley followed the raiders to Arkansas. There, he found no sign of Mary, who may have been killed or sold, but he did rescue George. Because he failed to bring Mary back, Bentley refused to take the land, but he did accept the $300 horse as payment for his services.

George and Jim were left with no living relatives. The Carvers gave them their freedom and decided to raise them as their own children. Jim was strong and able to work in the fields, while George, a sickly child, helped with the laundry, cleaned, cooked, and did other housework. Aunt Susan, as the boys called her, also taught George how to crochet and embroider.

8

A statue of Carver as a young boy sits in the woods at Carver National Monument in Diamond, Missouri.

The Plant Doctor

When he finished his chores each day, George slipped off to the woods, where he felt at home among the trees, plants, and ferns. He transplanted many of the species he discovered in the woods into a secret garden he planted. He began to study the plants, and tried to find answers to questions that puzzled him: Why did some plants, like clover, close up at night or on cloudy days? How could leaves on the same tree be different? Why did roots that looked exactly the same produce blossoms of different colors?

George planted flowers very close together to see if they would mix to produce new plants. He was puzzled when it did not work. If a plant appeared to be sick, he often dug deep into the soil to see if the roots were rotted or damaged.

He often brought home plants, rocks, reptiles, and insects, and sneaked them into the house so he could study them more carefully. Sometimes Susan found his collections and made him take them outside.

9

George had a natural instinct about plants and what they needed to grow and thrive. His ability to make plants flourish came mainly from his keen observations and experimentation. To determine what growing conditions worked best for different plants, he tested various combinations of sand, loam, and clay for potting soil, and also planted in locations with different amounts of shade and sunlight.

10

Carver lived in this house with his adoptive parents, Moses and Susan Carver.

He also learned how to inspect the foliage and blooms for insects, and observed which ones damaged the plants and which were beneficial. With this knowledge, he was able to figure out what was wrong with many of his neighbors' plants and nurse them back to health, which earned him the nickname, the Plant Doctor.

Carver attended an all-black school in Neosho, Missouri called the Lincoln School. It had only one room, similiar to the classroom pictured above.

An Enthusiastic Student

In 1872, when George was about eight years old, he asked Susan if he could go to school. Although the Carvers believed in education for all children, regardless of race, Missouri laws called for segregated schools, which did not allow children of different races to share the same classrooms. Sadly, she explained to the eager young boy that the nearby Locust Grove school was for white children only. The closest school for African American children was in Neosho, eight miles away.

Susan gave George a spelling book and helped him learn the alphabet. He was excited about learning how to spell and could not wait to go to school. He wanted to be a teacher. At eight years old, he was too young to leave home, but when he turned ten, the Carvers finally agreed that he could attend the one-room Lincoln School in Neosho. Because it was too far to walk to every day, and the Carvers had no horse to spare, they decided that George would have to find a new family to take him in, so he could live in Neosho.

A New Family

As he set out for Neosho, George was fearful of what lay ahead. The only home he had ever known was with the Carvers. Dressed in his best clothes, he walked very slowly as he carried most of his belongings, including his precious spelling book, in a small pack. By the time he got to town, it was dark, so he found a barn and crawled into the hayloft to sleep. It was there that the owner of the property, an African American woman named Mariah Watkins, found him the next day.

Like the Carvers, Watkins and her husband, Andrew, were childless. They told George that he could stay with them if he would help with the chores. Andrew worked as a gardener and handyman for many of the white families in town. To earn money, Mariah took in laundry. She also delivered babies and used her vast knowledge of medicinal plants and home remedies to care for the sick.

George often accompanied Mariah into the fields and woods to collect plant specimens for her work. She taught him the names of hundreds of plants and herbs and their many uses, as well as which roots, herbs, and bark to boil together to make medicines.

The Watkinses lived next door to the school, so during lunch hour and recess, George often went home to help wash and iron clothes. He also cut firewood, fed the chickens, gathered eggs, and milked the cow. If he had any free time between chores and school, he hired himself out to white families to earn extra money.

For the three years George lived with the Watkins family, he visited the Carvers on weekends whenever he had a chance. On most Sundays, he attended the African Methodist Church with Mariah and proudly carried the Bible she had given him.

George read his Bible and every other book that was available, eager to learn as much as he could. He even propped a book in front of him as he did the laundry or ironed the clothes, so he could read while he worked. He was a quick learner, and by the time he was 13, he realized that if he wanted to continue his education, he needed to leave Neosho. He had learned all he could at the Lincoln School.

Mariah Watkins taught Carver how to recognize hundreds of herbs and plants for medicinal use.

13

The Move to Fort Scott

Around this time, George heard that a local family was about to move to Fort Scott, Kansas, 75 miles away. They agreed to let him come along if he helped with the wagons on the long trip.

Although he was sad to leave the only friends and family he had ever known, he knew it was the right decision. Because Fort Scott was a larger community, it was certain to have a better school. Before he left, he had a picture taken with his brother, Jim. He gave a copy to the Watkinses and another to the Carvers, so they would remember him.

Over the next several years, George moved around Kansas and did whatever work he could find to pay for school. He had become more determined than ever to be a teacher. Whenever he had saved enough money, he went back to school. When he ran out of money, he would go back to work.

The Seymours, with whom he lived in Olathe, a small town in eastern Kansas, were especially kind to him. Lucy Seymour taught him how to iron garments with fancy ruffles and pleats in exchange for his help in the garden. He moved with the family to Minneapolis, Kansas, where he completed high school in 1884.

That same spring, he received word that his brother, Jim, had died the year before in Seneca, Missouri, of smallpox. After graduation, he decided to visit the Carvers and Watkinses. When he returned to Kansas, he used his savings from odd jobs to purchase land so he could start his own laundry. He hoped to earn enough money to go to college.

It was during this time that George acquired his middle name. A prolific letter writer, he often received mail from friends he had made in Missouri and Kansas, as well as from both of his sets of surrogate parents. He cherished those letters, which he read and reread. Because his mail was often delivered to another George Carver who lived in town, he added a "W" to his name as a middle initial. Whenever anyone asked what it stood for, he replied, "Washington."

A Fortunate Meeting

In spring 1884, when George Washington Carver was about 20 years old, he applied to Highland College, a small Presbyterian

At age 13, Carver moved to Fort Scott, Kansas, in order to get a better education.

school in Kansas. He was thrilled when he was accepted. He was ready to start classes in the fall, so it came as quite a shock when he arrived to register in September and was turned away because of his race. The school, he was told, did not accept African American students. After this rejection, Carver drifted from job to job, and eventually settled in Winterset, Iowa.

In Winterset, Carver resumed a practice he had always followed. He was a deeply religious man, but he did not belong to a particular church. Instead, he sought out the nearest house of worship or prayer meeting wherever he happened to be on Sundays. In Winterset, the nearest place of worship turned out to be a Methodist church. There, Carver met a white couple named John and Helen Milholland.

Helen Milholland was the church choir director. When she heard Carver sing in church, she asked her husband to invite him home. This was the start of a lifelong friendship.

While he lived in Winterset, Carver began to collect objects from nature, just as he had done as a boy. This time he did not simply admire them—he studied, identified, and classified them. He used bits of information he had learned from the books he had read over the years, and the occasional lectures he had attended.

Acceptance at Simpson College

The Milhollands were aware of Carver's never-ending quest for knowledge and would not allow him to abandon his dream of further education. In spring 1890, he was accepted at Simpson College, a Methodist school in Indianola, Iowa. That fall, after he paid off some business debts from his laundry, he packed up his belongings and walked 25 miles to the school to register. This time he was not turned away.

At Simpson, he wanted to study art, but his teachers tried to discourage him because they thought an art degree would not allow him to earn a living. Carver persisted, and finally, Etta Budd, the art director, granted him permission to attend art classes on a trial basis. She told him that he could participate for two weeks, at which time she would evaluate his work. If he showed any special talent, he would be allowed to continue. If not, he would have to withdraw from art class.

Carver was uneasy during those two weeks. He loved to draw and paint, but he was worried that Budd would decide he had no talent. At the end of the second week, she had not yet said anything to Carver. He finally gathered up the courage to approach her, and was greatly relieved when she agreed to let him stay in her class.

In the late nineteenth century, books and magazines illustrated plants and flowers—such as this one.

Art versus Science

Despite Carver's artistic talent, he never lost his curiosity about plants, and he often showed his art teacher specimens he had found in the woods, or had grown in pots in his room. He also liked to draw pictures of plants and flowers. When Budd noticed his keen interest, she encouraged him to consider a career in botany, the study of plants. Carver liked the idea. Finally, he could learn the answers to his questions about plants and how they grow.

Because Simpson did not offer the classes Carver needed to become a botanist, Budd contacted her father, Joseph Lancaster Budd, who was a professor of horticulture at Iowa State College of Agriculture and Mechanic Arts in Ames, Iowa. At the time, Iowa State was the top agricultural school in the country. Carver was reluctant to leave Simpson, where he had made many friends, but he realized that this was what he had to do. After less than a year at Simpson College, he transferred to Iowa State to study agricultural science, a course of study that included botany.

Etta Budd (center) with her family: her father, Joseph (left, seated); her brother, Allen (standing); and her mother, Sarah (right).

A New School

The move to the new college in 1891 was not an easy one. As the first African American student at Iowa State, he was called unkind names by some of the students, and ignored by others. He was not allowed to live in the same dormitory as the white students. Because there were no suitable accommodations for him, the college gave him an old office for his sleeping quarters. He was also expected to eat in the basement of the dining hall with the field hands. Carver found this treatment so humiliating that he almost quit school.

Carver (above) paints in an art class at Simpson College.

His situation improved when a friend from Indianola, an older white woman, visited him on campus. Her friendship with him opened the doors for his acceptance by the other students. Before long, he had made many friends.

A good student overall, Carver found some courses, such as botany, easier than others. He did not particularly like mathematics or history, although he worked hard to learn them.

In his botany class, he learned why his earlier experiments to mix, or crossbreed, plants had not worked. Planting the specimens close together was not the answer. A plant needed to receive pollen from another plant in order to produce new kinds of plants. Carver learned that if he carefully moved pollen from one plant to another by hand, he could create new plants of different colors and forms. He conducted most of his experiments on the amaryllis, one of his favorite flowers, and other plants grown from bulbs. He became very skilled at crossbreeding plants, and his professors noticed this ability.

In his agriculture classes, Carver learned how to apply science to farming, which gave him an insight into how plants grow and the unique relationship between plants and the soil. He saw what happened to plants when the soil lacked the minerals and nutrients they needed. He experimented with different amounts of potash, sulfur, and other minerals, and surprised everyone when he came up with a new artificial fertilizer that helped plants flourish.

In the spare time he had away from his work with plants, Carver painted them. In 1892, he exhibited four of his flower paintings at an art show in Cedar Rapids, Iowa. The judges were impressed by these works, and recommended that they be included at an exhibit at the World's Columbian Exposition in Chicago the following summer.

Carver (third row, fourth from left) was the first African American student to attend Iowa State University.

Carver (pictured above) won honorable mention for this yucca plant painting at the Chicago World's Fair (World's Columbian Exposition).

Carver entered a painting of a yucca plant. Much to his surprise, it earned an honorable mention at the exposition. Despite Carver's success as an artist, though, he never wavered in his decision to study botany.

First African American Graduate

Carver graduated in 1894 with a bachelor of science degree in agriculture. Because of his high grades and success in the crossbreeding of plants as a student, he was offered a position as an assistant botanist at the school's Agricultural Experiment Station. He was the first African American ever appointed to a teaching position at the school. In this job, Carver assisted Dr. Louis Pammell, a leading botanist and expert mycologist. He also taught classes and managed the campus greenhouses while he worked on his master's degree in agriculture and bacterial botany.

With Pammell's encouragement, Carver began to collect and study

Dr. Louis Pammell was a notable botanist and mycologist (fungi expert).

plant fungi as part of his training in mycology, at the time a relatively new field of scientific study, which focused on the growth of fungi. He built a collection of more than 20,000 specimens, including some new and rare fungi. Carver's keen observations and natural instincts about plants helped him discover fungi that no one else had found before. He knew that a plant wilted or grew poorly for a reason. Often it was because a fungus had attacked it.

While he was a student, Carver discovered a harmful fungus that grows on red and silver maple trees. It was named ***Taphrina carveri*** after him. He also became the first person to isolate a fungus that causes a serious disease in soybeans.

Carver and Pammell conducted experiments on fungal diseases of the cherry tree. The two men also studied rust, another plant fungus, which attacks a number of plant species, including blackberries, wheat, oats, and carnations. They worked together on two publications, ***The Treatment of Currants and Cherries to Prevent Spot Diseases and Fungus Diseases of Plants at Ames.***

Opposite: *Carver collected over 20,000 fungi specimens. He discovered fungi to be harmful to red and silver maple trees.*

Post-graduation Plans

Carver finished his master's degree in agriculture and bacterial botany in 1896. He was about 32 years old. Thanks in large part to his extensive research work, he was considered the best-trained African American agriculturist in the entire country. He also was a leading expert on fungal diseases of plants. It seemed obvious that he would choose an academic career, most likely at Iowa State.

After he had given the matter a lot of thought, he decided that he would pursue a career in agricultural education for five years. He thought he would like to establish an agricultural department, much like the one at Iowa State, at one of the African American schools that had been started in the South after the Civil War.

He had never lost his passion for art, however, so he also decided that after he had achieved his goal, he would return to painting. He thought he might enroll at the Art Institute of Chicago, if it would accept him as a student. Or perhaps he would go to Paris to study under one of the great French painters. In any event, Carver intended agricultural science to be only a temporary career before he pursued his dream of being an artist.

Carver's graduation photo.

Forty Acres and a Mule

Agriculture in the South was in terrible shape in the decades after the end of the Civil War. The problem was not that many of the plantation houses had burned down, or that the railroad tracks were torn up, but that the agricultural economy depended on only one crop: cotton.

Years of planting cotton in the same fields had taken a toll on the soil and deprived it of needed nutrients. Post-war advancements, such as better farm machinery, new planting methods, and

In the South, years of planting cotton in the same fields had taken a toll on the soil and deprived it of its nutrients.

improved transportation systems, could not help. Thus, although the industrialized North recovered quickly from the war, the agricultural South did not.

Many of the South's large plantations were carved up into smaller parcels of land after the Civil War ended. Some former slaves were given 40 acres and a mule to help them get a fresh start as freed men and women. Because most former slaves had worked on cotton plantations all their lives, they continued to plant cotton, even though yields were often poor, and they barely made enough money to buy fertilizer and seed for the following year.

The farmers needed help. If they were to survive, they had to receive the agricultural education that would help them become self-sufficient and financially stable. Carver, although he was not from the South, understood the problems that these farmers faced, and what they needed to do to solve their problems.

Invitation to Teach at Tuskegee

In 1896, Booker T. Washington, the founder of the Tuskegee Normal and Industrial Institute for Negroes in Tuskegee, Alabama, invited Carver to join his faculty. Washington needed someone to organize the new agricultural department at his school. At the time, Carver had been offered a teaching position at Alcorn Agricultural and Mechanical College in Mississippi, to which he gave serious consideration. Iowa State also wanted him to stay.

After he had corresponded with Washington for many months, Carver agreed to go to Tuskegee. He made it very clear to Washington that he planned to stay for only four or five years—just long enough to set up the department.

Arrival at Tuskegee

In October 1896, six months after he accepted the offer to teach at Tuskegee, Carver said goodbye to his friends in Ames and headed southeast to Alabama. Although Washington was anxious to have the agricultural scientist join his faculty, he had agreed to let Carver complete his research work for his master's degree in Iowa before he left for Tuskegee.

As Carver's train entered Alabama, the lush green scenery gradually gave way to fields of dry earth and "bumblebee cotton"—the

In 1896, Carver arrived at Tuskegee Institute, located on the site of an abandoned plantation.

nickname Southerners gave to the poor quality cotton that grew throughout the state. They said the plants were so stunted that a bee would barely need to fly to gather nectar from the blossoms..

Carver was dismayed by his first glimpse of the campus. He spotted scrub pines and yucca, but there were few flowers, shrubs, or grass. The parched clay soil was unlike the fertile landscape of Iowa State.

The campus, located on the site of an abandoned plantation, consisted of a few whitewashed wooden structures and some newer buildings that the students had constructed with clay bricks. Other buildings were still under construction. The dairy was nothing more than a single butter churn set up under a sweet gum tree. Carver wondered if he had made the right decision to come here.

"I cannot offer you money, position or fame. The first two you have. The last from the position you now occupy you will no doubt achieve. These things I now ask you to give up. I offer you in their place: work—hard, hard work, the task of bringing a people from degradation, poverty, and waste to full manhood."
—BOOKER T. WASHINGTON IN A LETTER TO GEORGE WASHINGTON CARVER

Tuskegee Institute.
Tuskegee, Ala. April 5th 1918.

A Makeshift Laboratory

Despite Carver's initial misgivings, he found that his 13 students were eager to learn about agriculture. Before he could begin, though, he had to set up a laboratory.

Because he had no supplies, except for a microscope that had been a gift from friends when he left Iowa, he sent his students into the community to find discarded items that could be turned into usable equipment for his makeshift laboratory. An old ink bottle became a Bunsen burner that could be used to heat experiments. Glass jars were used to store chemicals. Bottles were made into beakers. The new professor hated to see anything wasted, so he saved everything because he knew that he could probably reuse it someday.

Carver's microscope was given to him by friends when he left Iowa.

The agricultural building was under construction when he first arrived, so Carver conducted his classes in an unheated shack. Much of the land was swampy and covered with rubbish. With his students, Carver cleaned it up, then prepared the land to plant crops. He surprised his students when he said that they would plant cowpeas and velvet beans instead of cotton, the traditional crop of Alabama. He wanted to show the students how important it was to rotate crops, and to teach them that nitrogen-rich crops could improve soils that had been depleted of nutrients by years of growing the same crop.

Carver taught students that fertilized fields would produce higher crop yields. He knew that local farmers

In his lab at Tuskegee, Carver spent hours constructing and fixing tools he could use in his experiments.

most likely would not have extra money to spend on fertilizer, so he used materials that they would already have available—paper, rags, vegetable scraps, animal manure, and dead leaves—to make organic fertilizer, or compost.

To demonstrate his point, he took students to the campus dump, where kitchen food scraps and other debris were thrown away. There, a 37-foot pumpkin vine, with dozens of pumpkins on it, grew out of the trash heap. The huge plant had started from a discarded seed. The benefit of fertilization was one of the first of many ideas that Carver taught his students, ideas he had learned through his own education and research. He hoped to pass on these ideas to others.

A Gifted Teacher

Tuskegee may have lacked the fine facilities of his previous school, but Carver found that the students there were just as enthusiastic about learning as the students in Iowa had been. He knew that it was more effective to have students experiment and do real work than it was to teach with lectures alone. He began to take his botany classes on walks to study nature. He also brought native plants into the classroom for the students to examine closely.

"The study of nature is both entertaining and instructive, and it is the only true method that leads up to a clear understanding of the great natural principles which surround every branch of business in which we engage. Aside from this, it encourages investigation and stimulates originality."

—GEORGE WASHINGTON CARVER

Carver disagreed with the traditional methods used to teach botany, which included the memorization of long lists of scientific plant names without any real understanding of how plants were classified, or how they related to each other. From his early observations as a child, he knew that each plant had distinguishing characteristics. He knew plants with similar characteristics generally belonged to the same family.

Traditionally, students might learn the names of plants one year, how to grow them the next, and then study plant diseases and insects the year after that. This system made no sense to Carver. What good was it to know how to plant a fruit tree, he argued, if the student could not identify the insect pests that threatened its health?

He offered his students a more practical way to learn about plants. He grouped the plants by family to educate them about similarities among related species, as well as the insects and diseases that might attack them. He taught by demonstration and observation instead of lectures and textbooks. Soon, other students—even those who had previously scorned agricultural courses—wanted to attend his classes. By the time the school year ended in May 1897, 76 students, including 3 young women, had enrolled in his department.

Opposite: Carver became popular with students because of his innovative ideas about teaching.

Tuskegee Faculty

Although Carver was well liked by his students, many of his fellow professors resented him. Washington had recruited his other faculty members from his alma mater, Hampton Institute in Virginia, a school for African Americans. Hampton emphasized vocational skills to teach its students self-sufficiency. Carver, on the other hand, was a graduate of a prestigious white university. At Iowa State, students were taught academic subjects, such as mathematics, literature, and science.

Because he was better educated than the other faculty members, Carver received a salary of $125 per month. This was more than many of the other teachers made even after they had worked for several years at Tuskegee. They found this particularly insulting because the new teacher did not have a wife or children to support. He also demanded two dormitory rooms for his living quarters— one for him, the other for his growing collection of plant specimens, rocks, and fungi. This seemed like an unreasonable request to the faculty, since the other bachelor teachers lived two to a room.

The faculty members questioned why Washington would hire someone to teach agriculture. Most African Americans had done farm work all their lives, so what could a teacher show them that they did

Carver was resented by many of his fellow professors who had attended Hampton Institute, where vocational skills, not academics, were stressed.

not already know? Why give Carver such a high salary when the money could be better used in other departments, especially when he made it clear that he only intended to stay a few years?

The teachers were also appalled at the way Carver dressed. His wrinkled suit was faded and well worn in contrast to the fresh flower he always wore on his lapel. His shoes were scuffed and ready to fall apart. Comments about his clothes did not bother Carver, though. He never paid much attention to his appearance, because he believed that people were more interested in what he had to say than in what he wore.

Carver often wore wrinkled suits—but he always had a fresh flower on his lapel.

Carver's New Duties

When Carver accepted the position at Tuskegee, he did not realize that Washington expected him to teach a full course load, manage the school's two farms, and handle administrative duties, in addition to his research. Although he loved to teach, Carver thought he would be able to spend most of his time in his laboratory. There was a lot more that he wanted to learn about plants in order to help farmers.

Despite his desire to do research, during his first few years at Tuskegee, Carver instead organized the agriculture department, developed a curriculum, and taught students. He also landscaped the campus with native plants and grasses and recorded daily rainfall and other meteorological data for the weather bureau in Montgomery.

He did very little laboratory research and used most of his research efforts to set up field trials to teach his students and local farmers. He experimented with different crops, including sweet potatoes, to determine ideal growing conditions and ways to increase yield through soil improvements, such as fertilizer and crop rotation. For one demonstration, he planted five acres with a variety of crops to prove that it was possible to make a living from a small parcel of land.

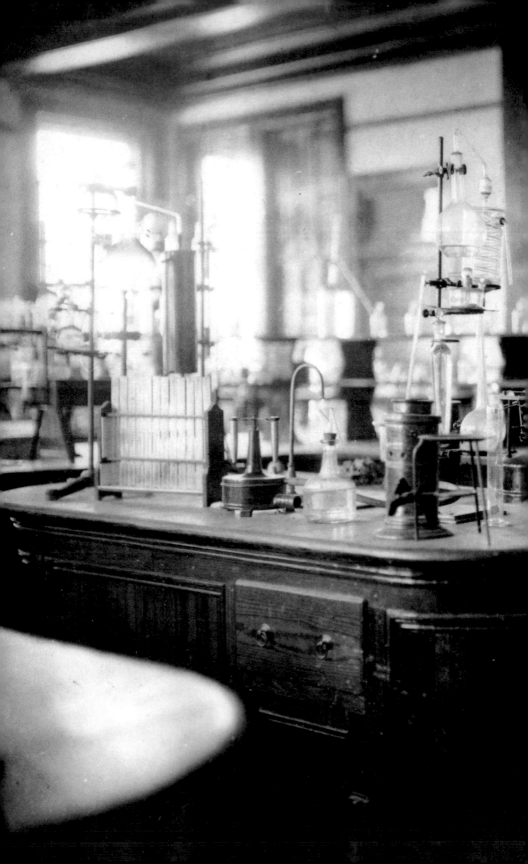

Though he always wanted more time in his laboratory, Carver did most of his research out in the fields. Here, he enjoys a rare opportunity to work in his Tuskegee lab.

Carver was in charge of five departments: dairy, farm management, livestock, vegetable farming, and horticulture. He also served as the school's veterinarian. When the Alabama legislature provided funds in 1897 to establish a research and experiment station at Tuskegee, Washington asked Carver to add "station director" to his other duties.

Carver wanted to help farmers improve the quality of the poor Alabama soil.

The purpose of the station was to "advance the interests of scientific agriculture." Carver wanted it to benefit Alabama's farmers directly. He intended for the station to provide research and education in several areas, including soil conservation, diversification of crops, new uses for traditional farm crops, and better use of native crops.

In 1899, in one of his earliest laboratory experiments, Carver found a way to extract rubber from a sweet potato. Although he was pleased with the results of his experiment, he was not sure it was worth investing more time on research. Not only was there small demand for rubber, but the little that was needed could be imported more cheaply than it could be manufactured. Rather than focus his attention on rubber, therefore, Carver devoted his time to his other research and his many duties at Tuskegee.

Going into the Community

Although Carver had many duties on campus, he was also expected to heed Washington's request that his faculty go out and teach the community to help improve the living conditions of rural people. Carver took this mission seriously. He often borrowed a horse from the stables and rode to neighboring towns in Macon County to meet the people he wanted to help.

Sometimes he brought bulletins with him that he had written to provide farmers with information, such as how to improve the soil or plant a garden. Many of these suggestions came from his research, reading, and observations. His first Tuskegee bulletin, which he wrote in 1899, focused on his

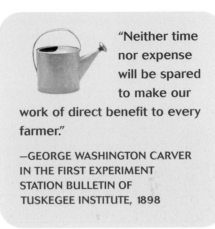

"Neither time nor expense will be spared to make our work of direct benefit to every farmer."

—GEORGE WASHINGTON CARVER
IN THE FIRST EXPERIMENT
STATION BULLETIN OF
TUSKEGEE INSTITUTE, 1898

investigation into feeding acorns to hogs. Because acorns contained many of the same food elements as corn, Carver assumed that acorns would fatten up hogs and that their meat would be tender. He found that the opposite was true, and he shared the results of his experiment with the farmers.

At times, Carver brought samples of fertilizer or equipment to demonstrate a new farming technique. Everything that he told the farmers, he had tried at the Tuskegee farm first to prove that it worked.

Initially, many farmers, both African American and white, were suspicious of Carver. His speech and mannerisms were more refined than theirs, and he spoke about things they knew nothing about. They wondered how a man from the Midwest could understand the problems of the South. He claimed to be a professor, but he did not look like one in his shabby suit with a flower on his lapel.

This curiosity about his background did not worry Carver. He knew that once he won people's trust, he could help them improve their farms.

Ideas about Gardens

One of Carver's biggest concerns was that most farmers planted cotton on every available foot of ground. They left no room for a vegetable garden, and chose instead to use the money from the sale of their crop to buy the food they needed. When the economy was poor and they did not get a good price for their cotton, they did not always have money to buy enough to eat.

Carver wanted to change that. He encouraged farmers to plant a variety of vegetables, and showed them how they could improve the soil if they added compost and fertilizer before they sowed the seeds. He taught women how to can and dry the crops harvested to make them last through the winter.

Carver found it harder to convince farmers to include edible wild plants in their diets. Many of the local people considered the plants he suggested, such as lamb's quarters, alfalfa, wild geranium, watercress, pokeweed, and chicory, to be roadside weeds. He quietly explained that they were good sources of vitamins and nutrients. This was a lesson he had learned as a child, when he lived with Mariah Watkins in Neosho.

Pigments from Clay

Carver also found ways to extract color pigments from clay soils for use as paint. He got the idea as he traveled around the county to talk to farmers. He was sad to see so many people living in unpainted, rundown shacks because they could not afford to fix them up.

To help them, he had to find a way to use materials that were readily available. As he looked around, he spotted deposits of multicolored clays. His artist's eyes saw deep reds, pale yellows, white, and cream colors. He wondered if there might be a way to remove those colors from the clays and use them as paint.

Carver took several buckets of clay back to his laboratory. He separated the clay according to color. Then, he scooped up a handful at a time and gently washed away the sand and stones until only the colored clay remained. He placed each sample in a canvas bag and used an iron to grind the clay into a fine powder. He mixed the powder with oil as well as hot and cold water, and he tested his paint on scraps of discarded wood. The colors were bright and did not fade, even when they were exposed to the sun and rain outdoors.

Carver tests paint that he made from different colored clays.

While he worked with the clays, he discovered faint traces of blue in a dark red clay sample. Through a process of adding oxygen at intervals, he was able to extract a beautiful bright blue powder whose hue was similar to the deep blue used by ancient Egyptians to decorate royal tombs. The house paints that Carver developed were more durable and of better quality than any of the commercial paints then available. They were also less expensive to produce. The scientist was eager to set up a factory on campus.

Washington, though he liked Carver's paints and even used them to paint some of the campus buildings, nevertheless turned down the request to create a paint factory. He told Carver that the institute lacked the resources to operate a factory once it was built. This was true, but Washington also knew that Carver did not have the administrative skills needed to run a business. Although he was an excellent teacher and researcher, Carver was a poor administrator. This was evident from his inability to manage the agricultural department and the faculty he supervised.

Carver with students in the Tuskegee chemistry lab. He was an excellent teacher.

Carver felt uncomfortable when he had to delegate work, and he did not know how to handle problems that arose within his department. Whenever he worked in his laboratory, he locked the door and made it clear that he was not to be disturbed. This angered many of the teachers, especially when Carver began to spend more time on his research than on his other assigned duties.

In 1904, Washington, who recognized that Carver might be happier at a larger university with better funding and more recognition for original research, suggested that he apply for a position at Carnegie Institute in Pittsburgh, Pennsylvania. Carver realized that Washington wanted to help, but he was not interested. He preferred to stay at Tuskegee, where he could continue to aid farmers both through research and education.

Washington wisely decided to relieve Carver of the duties he disliked, which gave him more time to do research. He asked Carver to continue to teach classes in chemistry and botany and to run the Agricultural Experiment Station. He also wanted Carver to provide outreach to farmers on their farms and through meetings on campus, including the Farmers' Conference, an annual field day and open house Washington had started 12 years before.

The Farmers' Institutes

Several hundred farmers and their wives attended this yearly event. Some came from as far as 50 miles away. The main purpose of the conference was to share results of Tuskegee's farm trials. Farmers might learn how compost use produced higher crop yields or how to make a living on a small plot of land. The farmers also had a chance to report on their own successes and failures. Carver listened carefully and took notes on the farmers' needs so that he could come up with new ways to help them.

The success of this annual open house led to monthly Farmers' Institutes. Once a month, farmers were invited to campus to view demonstration plots at the Tuskegee experimental farm and to learn about ongoing research in soil fertility, new crops, and other areas of agriculture.

At these meetings, Carver taught farmers about crop rotation and how they could improve the soil if they planted soybeans, peanuts, black-eyed peas, and velvet beans—just like he showed his students. He told them that these crops would add nitrogen to the soil to replace what had been lost during all the years when only cotton had been grown. He explained that the legumes he recommended take nitrogen from the air through their leaves and return it to the soil through their roots.

Even though the farmers could see from the farm trials that what Carver said was true, many were still skeptical. They had always been cotton growers, like their fathers before them. Besides, Carver had told them not to plant cotton and to let the soil rest, then make it rich again with other crops. They wondered how they would make any money while the land lay fallow.

Their initial reluctance led Carver to experiment with the hybridization of cotton plants to develop new and improved strains. "Carver's Hybrid" was his most successful, a cross between a tall-stalk strain with sturdy stems and a short-stalk cotton that produced fat bolls. The new strain was disease-resistant and had the best characteristics of both its parents.

"Carver's Hybrid" was a cotton crop that was a cross between tall- and short-stalk cotton.

"The primary idea in all of my work was to help the farmer and fill the poor man's empty dinner pail. My idea is to help the 'man farthest down.' This is why I have made every process just as simple as I could to put it within his reach."

—GEORGE WASHINGTON CARVER

Carver also used the meetings to discuss other ways to improve farmers' lives, such as eating a healthful diet. He was concerned because many farmers suffered from pellagra, a disease caused by a diet that consisted primarily of pork, molasses, and cornmeal.

Carver wanted them to eat more nutritious foods, like the ones Mariah Watkins had taught him about in Neosho many years ago, and those he had learned about at Iowa State and in books. He developed new recipes for the farm families to try, and asked the home economics teachers at Tuskegee to demonstrate how to prepare healthful foods.

The Movable School

To expand his efforts in an attempt to reach farmers, Carver drew up plans for what he called a movable school. He envisioned a demonstration wagon equipped with agricultural exhibits that would travel around the state on a regular schedule to educate farmers about new ideas and techniques.

The Jesup Agricultural Wagon, as it became known, was a horse-drawn vehicle named for Morris K. Jesup, the New York banker who provided most of the money for it. Students at Tuskegee built the wagon in 1906. Carver asked Thomas Campbell, one of his best students, to operate it, so he, himself, could spend more time in his laboratory.

Campbell might load the wagon with a cream separator, purebred hog, or high-production milk cow for the demonstrations. He often gathered farmers together at one farm to demonstrate planting or plowing techniques, such as the use of a two-horse plow instead of a single horse and plow, which allowed fields to be tilled quicker. At harvest time, the Jesup Wagon would carry a load of produce grown in the Tuskegee Institute's fields.

Sometimes, Carver went along to share his tips on how to grow prize vegetables and fruits, techniques he had learned from his work

Thomas Campbell, Carver's assistant, taught farmers that using a one-horse plow was less efficient than using a two-horse plow.

Thomas Campbell in the lab.

Carver taught women how to preserve food, as well as how to weave mats from reeds, string, or burlap. He also showed them how to make laundry starch: He placed peeled, grated sweet potatoes in a cheesecloth bag, dipped it in water and squeezed, then repeated the process until no more liquid came out and only the starch remained. The movable agricultural school was so successful that the U.S. Department of Agriculture later adopted the idea.

A Threat to Cotton

By the early 1900s, many farmers had begun to listen to Carver, but most still wanted to plant cotton. It was all that they knew. Then, at the beginning of the twentieth century, something happened that made them change their minds. The boll weevil, a devastating insect pest from Mexico, advanced into Texas and began to feed on the cotton crop there. Over the next decade, the beetle slowly made its way through the South. By 1911, it had become a problem for cotton farmers in Alabama.

For years, Carver had recommended that farmers plant more than one market crop, in case of just such a disaster. They were finally ready to listen. He encouraged them to grow peanuts, a crop well adapted to the soil, climate, and growing conditions of the South.

New Uses for Peanuts

Many of the farmers in the county followed Carver's advice and planted peanuts. Their yields were high, but there was not enough demand for the new crop in a state where cotton had always been king. Surplus peanuts rotted in sheds, and the farmers were furious with Carver. He became worried. The farmers were right—it was his fault. He blamed himself because he had not thought his idea through completely.

He took a long walk in the woods to pray, as he often did when he was faced with a problem to solve. When he returned, he locked

Following Carver's advice, many Southern farmers planted peanuts instead of cotton.

himself in his laboratory and began to experiment with peanuts. For several days, he did not leave the laboratory, and he barely touched the food his students brought for him. When he finally emerged, he was exhausted, but triumphant.

Carver had made use of his knowledge of chemistry and physics to separate the water, fats, oils, sugars, starches, and other components of the peanut. He then experimented with different combinations of those parts, and subjected them to various temperatures and pressures.

In one experiment, he ground the peanuts into powder, which he heated and then squeezed with a hand press until a smooth oil dripped out. Carver found that he could mix the oil with pigments, fragrances, and other substances to make soap, shampoo, hand lotion, shaving cream, and other products. The extract also made a good cooking oil that could be used to fry foods.

Within one week, the researcher also came up with several other new uses for peanuts, including milk, cheese, buttermilk, instant coffee, and other foods. He was especially excited about the peanut milk, which he believed was a delicious, nutritious, and inexpensive source of protein. He could make a pint of milk from only three ounces of nuts, and he boasted that the way he made milk was quicker and more efficient than the way a cow did it.

His success made farmers happy, but Carver knew that he also had to convince the area businesspeople of the economic value of his peanut products. He invited them to campus for lunch. He served soup, mock chicken, creamed vegetables, greens, bread, salad, cookies, candy, ice cream, and coffee. When he informed the diners that everything, except the greens, was made from peanuts, they were astounded. He quickly won their support.

Washington was pleased with Carver's progress and encouraged him to continue his research. Despite the fact that resources at the institute were limited, Washington tried to respond favorably to the scientist's requests for equipment and materials. He also spoke highly of Carver's work when he went on speaking tours in the North to raise money for Tuskegee Institute.

In the fall of 1915, Washington collapsed during a fundraising tour in New Haven, Connecticut. He returned to Tuskegee, where he died on November 14. He was 50 years old.

The New Principal

Although people of all races mourned Washington's passing, no one grieved more than Carver. The two men may have disagreed at times on matters that involved the Tuskegee Institute, but they had become friends over the years. They shared the same vision, in which they hoped to improve the lives of the students and the community, particularly African American farmers.

The death of his friend upset Carver so much that he lost all interest in research. He locked himself in his room for days at a time and refused all visitors. When he did step out, he wandered aimlessly about campus and showed no interest in his surroundings.

In the spring of 1916, Carver began to visit The Oaks, Washington's former home. It was now occupied by Washington's son, David-son, and his wife. To cheer Carver up, she told him that her father-in-law had come to her in a dream and told her, "Professor Carver will carry on for me. I have faith in him." Carver felt better when he heard this. Before long, he decided to return to his laboratory.

Booker T. Washington was one of Carver's closest friends and his most supportive colleague.

By then, a new principal, Robert Russa Moton, had been selected to replace Washington. Much to Carver's delight, Moton was willing to relieve him of most of his teaching responsibilities. He only asked that Carver continue to teach summer school. He agreed. The summer session provided advanced instruction to African American schoolteachers, which Carver felt was worthy of his time.

Carver no longer taught during the regular semesters, but he continued to take a personal interest in the students, and invited them to drop by his rooms to chat. He also led a Bible class that was more popular than many of the organized religious classes and chapel services held on campus.

War Department Invitation

With more time to devote to his research, Carver began to focus on ways to develop new products from peanuts and other foods, such as sweet potatoes and soybeans. One of his experiments, in which he made flour from sweet potatoes, came to the attention of the U.S. government during World War I (1914–1918). The government wanted to find a substitute for wheat, which was in short supply because of the war.

The U.S. government became interested in Carver's flour made from sweet potatoes because of the shortage of wheat flour during World War I.

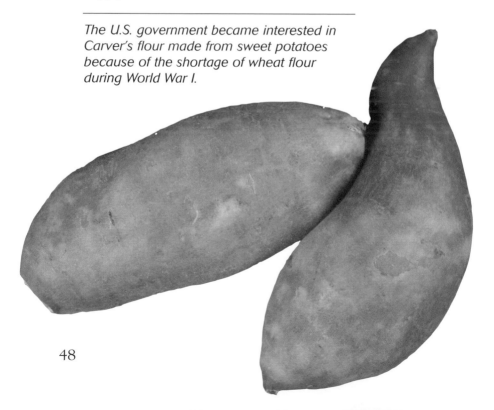

48

The War Department was excited to learn that the Tuskegee Institute had found a solution to the wheat shortage. Thanks to Carver, the institute saved up to two pounds of wheat a day when it substituted sweet potato flour for regular baking flour.

In early 1918, the War Department invited Carver to Washington, D.C., to demonstrate how to make his sweet potato flour. Carver showed army cooks how to make the flour with a process that steamed the sweet potatoes until they were soft, then sliced and mashed them by hand or with a food chopper. Carver explained how to dry the sweet potato mash until it was brittle, then grind it in a food mill to make a powder. He then sifted that powder through a finely woven cloth, collected the fine particles that passed through the cloth, and discarded the coarser granules that were left on the surface. The fine particles that remained became the flour.

Carver not only taught army cooks how to make bread from sweet potato flour, but he showed them how to dry fruits and vegetables. He also taught them how to make coffee and egg substitutes. He was flattered by all the attention. He shared his information freely, and asked for nothing—no money, no patents, and no manufacturing rights. When the war ended later that year, the government showed no further interest in Carver's products, much to his disappointment.

Back home in Alabama, peanuts had slowly begun to replace cotton. Yet despite high production, and the increased interest of farmers in this crop, peanuts were still imported from Africa.

The United Peanut Association

The United Peanut Association of America, which was established to promote peanuts, met in September 1920 to discuss its concerns and push for a high tax to keep African peanuts out of the country. Its members invited Carver to demonstrate his peanut products.

Carver took the train to Montgomery, Alabama, where the association was scheduled to meet at the Exchange Hotel. The doorman, unaware that an African American had been invited to speak to the all-white group, refused to let him enter the hotel. He even lied and told Carver that the association had moved its meeting place to the city hall. When Carver arrived there, he was informed that the meeting was, in fact, at the hotel.

Carver finally gained admittance after he handed the doorman a note to deliver to the president of the association. When the doorman returned, he directed Carver to the service entrance. Carver was deeply humiliated but knew that he had to speak, not only for the sake of farmers, but also to gain recognition for the products he had developed.

As soon as he began to speak, he had the undivided attention of his audience, who were fascinated by the many products he had made from peanuts. He showed them different kinds of peanut milk, cream, fruit punch, instant coffee, and stains for wood and leather, and he explained that these were only a small sample of the many uses of peanuts. When he finished his speech, the association was convinced that Carver was the man to represent its interests in Washington, D.C.

Passage of Fordney-McCumber Tariff Bill

The success of his talk led to an invitation in January 1921 to testify before the House Ways and Means Committee of the U.S. House of Representatives in favor of a tariff to protect peanuts and other agricultural products from foreign competition. By that time, more than one-fourth of the country's peanuts were grown in Alabama.

Carver's presentation helped convince legislators to vote in favor of the tariff. This was a major economic boon for the $200 million-a-year peanut industry. The bill became known as the Fordney-McCumber Tariff Act.

The bill may have helped agricultural producers such as Alabama's peanut farmers, but in the long term, it hurt world trade. The high tariffs meant fewer foreign imports. This boosted sales of American goods, including agricultural products. Because America did not want their products, however, these foreign countries no longer bought from the United States, which upset the economy.

On the other hand, the tax created such a strong demand for American-produced peanuts that peanut farmers no longer worried that they would have a surplus. They found instead that they could not grow enough peanuts to meet the demand. Although Carver continued to develop new products from peanuts, he soon shifted his focus and worked to find additional uses for soybeans, sweet potatoes, pecans, and other crops.

Carver was called the "Wizard of Tuskegee" because he developed so many products from peanuts and sweet potatoes.

The Wizard of Tuskegee

After Carver's success in Washington in 1921, invitations to speak began to pour in for the man the newspapers had dubbed the "Wizard of Tuskegee." Many of these requests came from white colleges and organizations.

Carver would have preferred to remain in his laboratory, but he realized that these speaking engagements were a good way to break down racial barriers, while he also shared his scientific discoveries. By this time, he had developed hundreds of products from farm produce, including shoe polish, bleach, talcum powder, paper, metal polish, axle grease, and synthetic rubber. He also created food products, such as mayonnaise, meat tenderizer, and chili sauce.

These accomplishments brought Carver national recognition. In the fall of 1923, Carver was named the recipient of the prestigious Spingarn Medal, awarded annually by the National Association for the Advancement of Colored People (NAACP). He received it for his pioneering work in the field of agricultural chemistry, including his invention of more than 300 products from peanuts, as well as for his efforts to put his knowledge and research to work for the benefit of his race.

Despite all the interest in his work, Carver applied for patents for only three of his products and processes. The U.S. Patent Office granted him two patents in 1925, one for a process that made cosmetics from peanuts, and the other for multiple processes to manufacture paints and stains from clay and minerals. Two years later, he received a third patent, for a cold-water process to produce paints and stains from soybeans.

Carver could have made a lot of money from his discoveries, but he always insisted that God guided him, so his inventions belonged to the people. He did not want to see them patented. "God gave them to me," he often said. "How can I sell them to someone else?"

Two Great Minds

In the early 1920s, Carver's work came to the attention of inventor Thomas Alva Edison, who hoped to find a source of American rubber. Although the Alabama scientist had created a sweet potato rubber many years earlier, at that time, rubber could be imported cheaply, so he never tried to market it.

Edison thought sweet potato rubber had great possibilities and invited Carver to work for him at his West Orange, New Jersey, laboratory for a reported six-figure salary, a phenomenal sum of money for the time. In addition, Edison mentioned Carver's work to Henry Ford, an automobile manufacturer in Michigan, who was also interested in new sources of rubber. Neither man could convince Carver to leave Tuskegee for any amount of money.

A Generous Spirit

Carver was very generous with his money, and he gave 10 to 20 percent of his salary to charitable causes and individuals. Because he remembered how difficult it had been for him to find enough money to stay in school, he was quick to lend students money to help them continue their education.

Henry Ford (left) tried unsuccessfully to convince Carver to leave Tuskegee to work with him on sweet potato rubber.

He spent almost nothing on himself, and wore the same comfortable, worn-out clothes when he entertained important guests, such as visiting U.S. presidents, that he wore when he worked in his laboratory. Not only was he frugal, but he seemed to have little regard for money. He never asked for a raise or accepted one, and he often forgot to cash his paychecks. In his later years at Tuskegee, many of his assistants made more money than he did.

In the 1930s, he lost more than $30,000 during the Great Depression, a period of economic upheaval and widespread unemployment caused by a stock market crash in 1929. The loss of most of his savings did not upset Carver. His lack of concern at the time was partly because he was preoccupied with his research. He believed that he might have found a cure for infantile paralysis, also known as polio. It was time to test his theory.

A Cure for Infantile Paralysis

Carver noticed when peanut oil was used as rubbing lotion, it helped to ease soreness and pain more quickly than commercially available products. He was also convinced that peanut oil could improve muscles that were wasted by polio, and help patients gain weight.

In late 1932, Carver proved his theory when he began to help two local boys who had the disease. Through weekly massages, he gradually improved their muscle tone and actually helped one boy walk again. News of the child's amazing recovery spread quickly through Alabama, and people began to travel many miles for treatment, because they believed Carver had found a cure.

In December 1933, an article in the *Montgomery Advertiser* announced that Carver, then about 69 years old, had indeed found a cure for infantile paralysis that used peanut oil massages. The article was picked up by the Associated Press wire service. Soon, hundreds of letters from all over the world began to arrive at Carver's office. Although he tried to answer them all, eventually there were so many that a secretary was assigned to him for several months, just to answer his mail.

Carver hated to turn anyone away, but too many people wanted his help. His own health was poor, and his doctor warned him that if he continued to work so hard, he would damage his already weakened heart. Moton was concerned for Carver's health, but he was also worried that if something happened to the scientist, much of his work would be lost forever, because he rarely wrote down anything. Moton wanted Carver to train an assistant who could carry on his work after he was gone.

God's Little Workshop

Carver scoffed at the idea of an assistant, and said, "Only alone can I draw close enough to God to discover His secrets." He even referred to his laboratory as "God's Little Workshop."

Carver was also very secretive about his research. He always worked alone, and he allowed no witnesses when he conducted his experiments. He seldom recorded anything, and relied on his memory to recall the steps when he needed them. He found it time-consuming to write everything down.

Despite Carver's protests, Moton often assigned him assistants, whom Carver usually ignored or dismissed. In 1935, he finally found someone he liked: Austin W. Curtis, a chemistry graduate from Cornell University. Because he did not want an assistant, Carver told the young man that he would let him know when he was needed. Curtis waited for a long time, but Carver never asked him to come to the laboratory. Curtis decided instead to conduct his own experiments with plant materials.

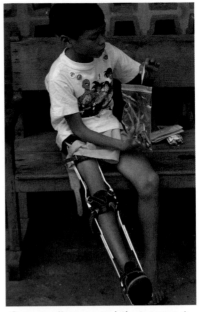

Carver discovered that peanut oil could be used to treat polio in children.

Carver's curiosity soon got the better of him, and one day, as Curtis explored different ways to extract oil from magnolia seeds to use for soap, Carver visited his young assistant's laboratory. The two talked, and Carver realized that Curtis shared many of his interests, including a strong desire to improve the lives of Alabama's farmers. After that day, they were inseparable friends.

In 1935, Frederick D. Patterson became the new head of Tuskegee after Moton resigned. Patterson thought Carver and his work provided great publicity for the institute, and he was willing to continue to fund Carver's research and outreach work with farmers. The following year, to honor Carver, he declared the 1936–1937 school year to be Carver Anniversary Year, in recognition of the scientist's 40 years at the Tuskegee Institute.

Patterson asked Carver to set up an exhibit that highlighted his achievements. The scientist included everything—early wood-carvings, pottery, lacework, paintings, scientific bulletins, and his collections of rocks, plants, fungi, and animals, as well as products made from peanuts, sweet potatoes, pecans, soybeans, and Alabama clays. The exhibit was so well received that in 1937, the institute's board of trustees voted to establish the George Washington Carver Museum. Carver was delighted.

A Dream Is Achieved

By the fall of 1937, Carver's health began to fail, and he was hospitalized for several months after he collapsed in the school's dining hall. Carver suffered from exhaustion and anemia. The doctors did not think he would recover, but he did, and he returned to campus, though his declining health did not allow him to conduct any serious research.

Instead, Carver now devoted his time to the establishment of a foundation with research facilities and funding for scientists to continue his work in agricultural research. With the help of his assistant, Curtis, he tried to raise enough money to start the foundation.

Despite Carver's prominence in the scientific community and his great public appeal, contributions only trickled in and never reached the set goal. In 1940, Carver decided to contribute several thousand dollars from his own savings account. The Tuskegee Institute donated the former campus laundry building, which contained a crude laboratory in the basement. Finally, Carver's dream—the George Washington Carver Foundation—became a reality.

Carver also decided to set up the museum approved by the board of trustees, and for three years, beginning in 1938, he gave much of his time to this project. He was concerned that if he let someone else do it, his collections would not be organized properly.

Although he was frustrated by delays and his own waning energy, Carver continued to struggle to get his museum started. More than 2,000 people attended the opening day on July 25, 1939. Public interest prompted Carver to expand the museum, and the expansion was completed in 1941.

During this time, Carver worked with Curtis on a few minor research projects, but he depended on his assistant to handle most of the work. He accepted few speaking engagements, but did return to Simpson College in June 1941 to speak to the graduating class.

He was also eager to convince the medical profession to accept his peanut oil massages as a legitimate treatment for polio, even though many people were skeptical that Carver had really found a cure. He consulted with doctors and therapists throughout the country, including those who worked at the Tuskegee Infantile Paralysis Center. The center had been established on campus in 1941 to provide care for African Americans with polio.

Carver—in his greenhouse—worked well past retirement age.

Carver's Legacy Continues

Carver continued to work long past an age by which most men and women would have retired. This surprised many people because he had always said that one day, he wanted to give up research to return to his painting. He never did, although he continued to paint as a hobby throughout his life.

Carver's health continued to decline, and when he felt weak one day in mid-December 1942, he took to his bed. He never recovered. Carver died on January 5, 1943. He was buried in the campus cemetery next to Booker T. Washington. He was around 80 years old.

Carver never married, so he had no heirs. In his will, he requested that his life savings be given to the George Washington Carver Foundation to help fund Tuskegee scientists involved in agricultural research, especially those who explored new uses for plant-based resources, as he had done for more than five decades.

Carver's work with farmers revolutionized Southern agriculture in the early part of the twentieth century and made it possible for small-scale farmers to survive. He also helped lay the groundwork for future scientific discoveries and industrial research that used renewable resources, including food crops.

Before Carver made his discoveries, few people had considered the use of agricultural products for anything other than food and clothing. He saw these resources as building blocks that could be used to create many new products. By the time of his death in 1943, he had developed more than 300 products from peanuts and more than 100 from sweet potatoes. He also found dozens of other creative uses for crops, such as cotton, pecans, and soybeans. Many more recent advancements in agricultural science and technology have been possible, in part, because of Carver's vast, forward-thinking scientific contributions.

"When Dr. Carver died the United States lost one of its finest Christian gentlemen. To the world he was known as a scientist. Those who knew him best, however, realize that his outstanding characteristic was a strong feeling of the eminence of God. Everything he was and did found origin in that strong and continuous feeling."

—HENRY A. WALLACE, VICE PRESIDENT OF THE UNITED STATES

Opposite: *Carver performed many experiments on crossbreeding varieties of plants. His favorite subject was the amaryllis.*

IMPORTANT DATES

c. 1864 George Carver is born to a slave named Mary near Diamond Grove, Missouri.

1865 Slave raiders abduct young Carver and his mother; only the boy is found and returned to Moses and Susan Carver.

1872 Susan Carver gives Carver his first spelling book.

1881 Booker T. Washington establishes Tuskegee Normal and Industrial Institute for Negroes in Tuskegee, Alabama.

1883 James Carver, George's older brother and only known living relative, dies.

1884 Carver is accepted at Highland College in Highland, Kansas, but is later turned away because of his race.

1890 Carver enters Simpson College in Indianola, Iowa.

1891 Carver transfers to Iowa State College of Agriculture and Mechanic Arts in Ames, Iowa.

1892 Booker T. Washington holds the first annual Farm Conference, a field day and open house at Tuskegee Institute.

1893 Four of Carver's paintings are chosen for exhibition at the World's Columbian Exposition in Chicago.

1894 Carver graduates from Iowa State College and becomes the first African American ever appointed to the faculty.

1896 Carver receives a master's degree from Iowa State College. Carver begins teaching at the Tuskegee Institute.

1897 The Alabama State Legislature establishes a research station at Tuskegee; Carver serves as its first director.

1906 Carver and Thomas Campbell, a Tuskegee student, first take their "movable school" to Macon County farmers.

1911 The boll weevil, a devastating cotton pest, makes its way into Alabama.

1915 Booker T. Washington dies at age 50.

1918 The U.S. government invites Carver to Washington, D.C., to demonstrate how to make sweet potato flour. Carver is appointed a consultant to the U.S. Department of Agriculture.

1920 The United Peanut Association of America invites Carver to demonstrate his peanut products at its meeting in Montgomery, Alabama.

1921 Carver testifies before the Ways and Means Committee of the U.S. House of Representatives in favor of a tariff to protect agricultural and industrial products from foreign competition.

1922 The Fordney-McCumber Tariff Bill is passed.

1923 The National Association for the Advancement of Colored People (NAACP) awards Carver the Spingarn Medal for his contributions in the field of agricultural chemistry.

1925 Carver is issued two patents: one for a process to make cosmetics from peanuts, and another for several processes to manufacture paints and stains from clay and minerals.

1927 Carver is issued a patent for a process to produce paints and stains from soybeans.

1933 An article in the *Montgomery Advertiser* announces that Carver has found a cure for infantile paralysis that uses peanut oil massages.

1935 Austin W. Curtis becomes Carver's assistant.

1936 To honor Carver's fortieth year at Tuskegee, the institute declares the 1936–1937 school year to be the Carver Anniversary Year.

1937 Carver is hospitalized for several months, and suffers from exhaustion and anemia.

1938 The Tuskegee board of trustees votes to establish the George Washington Carver Museum.

1939 The Carver Museum first opens to the public.

1940 The George Washington Carver Foundation is created at Tuskegee Institute to support agricultural research.

1941 The expansion of the George Washington Carver Museum is completed.

1943 George Washington Carver dies.

GLOSSARY

Abolitionist: someone who opposes slavery and would like to see it eliminated

Amaryllis: any bulbous plant, usually with large, showy flowers, of the genus *Amaryllis* of the family *Amarylidaceae*

Anemia: a condition in which the blood does not have enough red blood cells, which may cause weakness and tiredness

Boll: seed-bearing capsule of certain plants, especially cotton and flax

Boll weevil: a tiny, gray, long-nosed beetle found in Mexico and the southern United States

Botanist: a scientist who specializes in the study of plants

Botany: the scientific study of plant life

Bumblebee cotton: what Southerners called the poor-quality cotton grown on nutrient-deficient soil, so named because a bee would barely need to fly to gather nectar from the low-growing blossoms

Bunsen burner: a gas burner used in laboratories that has an air valve to regulate the mixture of gas and air

Chemurgy: the development of new industrial chemical products from organic raw materials, especially from those of agricultural origin

Commodities: an article of trade or commerce, especially an agricultural or mining product that can be processed and resold

Compost: a mixture of decaying plant and organic matter used to fertilize and improve the condition of the soil

Crop rotation: a way to conserve soil fertility by planting different crops with different nutrient requirements on the same soil in successive years

Crossbreed: to mix or interbreed two varieties of the same species

Curriculum: set of courses offered by a school or educational institution.

Diversification: the act of introducing variety

Fallow: cultivated land left idle during the growing season

Horticulture: the science or art of growing fruits, vegetables, flowers, or ornamental plants

Hybridization: the act of producing a new organism by the mating of individuals of different breeds, varieties, or species

Import: to bring or carry in from an outside source, especially to bring in goods or materials from a foreign country for trade or sale

Legume: the fruit or seed of a plant of the *Leguminosae* family, such as peas, beans, or lentils

Loam: a type of soil that consists of clay, sand, and silt

Mycology: the scientific study of fungi

Nutrient: a source of nourishment, especially a nourishing ingredient in a food or plant

Patent: a grant made by a government that gives the creator of an invention the sole right to make, use, and sell that invention for a set period of time

Pellagra: a disease caused by a deficiency of niacin and protein in the diet, which causes skin eruptions, problems with food digestion, nervousness, and eventual mental deterioration

Pigment: a substance that imparts color to other materials

Pollen: a mass of microspores in a seed plant

Synthetic: something that is artificially made rather than natural

Tariff: a tax put on imported goods

Yucca: any of various evergreen plants of the genus *Yucca*, native to the warmer regions of North America, often having tall, strong stems and a cluster of white flowers at the end of the stem

FOR MORE INFORMATION

BOOKS

Benge, Janet and Geoff Benge. Kennon James (Illustrator). *George Washington Carver, What Do You See?* Houston, TX: Advance Publishing, 1997.

Benitez, Mirna. Meryl Henderson (Illustrator). *George Washington Carver, Plant Doctor.* Milwaukee, WI: Raintree Publications, 1989.

Mitchell, Barbara. Peter E. Hanson (Illustrator). *A Pocketful of Goobers: A Story about George Washington Carver.* Minneapolis, MN: Carolrhoda Books, 1986.

Nelson, Marilyn. *Carver: A Life in Poems.* Asheville, NC: Front Street, 2001.

WEB SITE

Legends of Tuskegee
Learn about George Washington Carver from his early years as a slave to his rise to fame as a great scientist, teacher, and leader at Tuskegee Institute—www.cr.nps.gov/museum/exhibits/tuskegee

INDEX